David Zwirner Books   *ekphrasis*

On Contemporary Art
César Aira

Translated by Katherine Silver

Contents

Foreword

Will Chancellor

My first memory of being defeated by language was in my mom's car, as I read the puzzle of words printed on the side mirror: OBJECTS IN MIRROR ARE CLOSER THAN THEY APPEAR. I had just graduated to the front seat and would spend the remainder of this road trip looking at trees tick past, checking how they appeared in the mirror, then tracking them until they disappeared. I couldn't understand how objects and their appearance could possibly diverge. What was this new logic of images? Did adults live with constant reminding of the gap between reality and what they could see?

César Aira begins his essay "On Contemporary Art" by postulating that this gap between appearance and reality might be the genesis of classical art (meaning, for him, all art before Marcel Duchamp). Aira first asks us to imagine a Paleolithic tribe huddled in a cave. Firelight flickers on a cave painting of a hunt. Perhaps different angles and intensities from fire in a pit, or a waved torch, patter the legs of the bison into something like a trot. But we're a long way from animation, much less cinema. No matter how interesting the image on the wall, the painting of the hunt lacks the feeling of the hunt. It's just … flat. Enter the storyteller.

The storyteller's job is to translate, not transcribe, events. The facts at hand—"There was a bison; we threw spears into its body until it fell"—are merely the pretext for the story, and not the story itself. A related experience will lull a crowd to sleep, but if the storyteller can make the hunt *happen* again, right there in the cave, then people will come from the other side of the hill to hear about it. Aira writes, "The mediation of images imposes a distance, and that distance opens up a space in which words can resonate and multiply their expression beyond what is utilitarian." I'd like to stress the importance of reading Aira visually when he describes the distance between an art object and how it appears to a viewer. By visualizing these distances, a reader can feel the spatial tension in art, a tension akin to a well-tuned violin string's resonant note.

Coincidentally, in depicting the gap between observer and observed, Aira provides an excellent definition for "ekphrasis" itself. Describing an art object is not a utilitarian task. Rather than attempt to bring us closer and closer to the art object until we asymptotically approach the thing itself, transcendent ekphrastic writing, like Homer's relation of Achilles's shield, holds the object at a constant distance. To see Achilles's shield with the full charge that sight must have generated for someone on a Trojan shore, a poet must hold it close enough in the mind's eye to see the wedding playing out on the shield's surface, but also keep it at enough of a remove to recognize the oceanic designs around the rim. When artist and writer effectively manage this timeless distance, a viewer or reader can inhabit the work.

This mediated distance between artwork and reality is, however, only the first of several distances Aira cites in our relationship to art. With the advent of photography, the gap in classical art, which formerly allowed "productive fantasizing," closed. Contemporary art, on the other hand, distinguishes itself by staying one step ahead of reproduction. Aira describes the experience of paging through *Artforum* and finding "an increasingly impoverished and disheartening visual display." At first, this seems like condemnation, but in context we see that art magazines are blameless, and possibly deserving of praise for highlighting exactly what contemporary art is—that which can never be adequately reproduced on the page. Therefore, we turn to contemporary art with excitement because there is room here for a story. Aira imagines a pile of sand on a gallery floor and thinks, "It could be sand from Sinai transported to a museum in Alaska, or the idea is for the spectators to spread it around, or sit on it, or each should take a grain, or it could be covering a Constantin Brancusi sculpture … You cannot photograph a concept." An artist's statement often comes across as a weak text, necessarily failing to capture all the untold stories in the act of telling only one. Here, literature serves as "the silver bridge hung between the done and the not-done." And what use are bridges when there's no gap?

It's hard to imagine anyone today writing an essay in praise of distance. Our default mode is acquisitive, grasping, wanting to have everything at hand. A friend tells you about his long-distance relationship and you can't help but grimace and wonder how he got this far in life without knowing that never works. Another friend leaves for a two-week vacation and you feel obliged to throw a homecoming party, as if she's miraculously returned from the underworld. Reading César Aira's essay has me excited again about the potential inherent in distance—the ability to keep an image at a static remove and create stories in the gap rather than heed the imperative of *Closer, get closer, and closer still*. More than anything else, the vision articulated here reminds me of Yasujirō Ozu's films and the narrative possibilities created by a camera looking at a room, head on, from a fixed distance. The creative restraint on the part of the director, or artist, or writer, to refuse to zoom in on the image at hand in turn creates a space for an infinite number of narratives. The trick is to find a way into that small, ever-diminishing gap and, as Aira says, "write the footnotes."

On Contemporary Art

César Aira
Translated by Katherine Silver

My perspective is that of a writer who looks for inspiration, stimulation, means, and themes in painting. In other words, a classical character, almost conventional, and almost inevitable. One possible beginning of the history of literature—an origin myth, at any rate—could be of the first poem or the first story as a mythical description or interpretation of a drawing or a statue. Telling friends or cave neighbors how I hunted a bison is a simple act of communication, where language is purely functional; but telling them the story evoked by the bison and the hunters painted on the wall ... that could well be a harbinger of literature. The mediation of images imposes a distance, and that distance opens up a space in which words can resonate and multiply their expression beyond what is utilitarian.

As an origin myth, it is fairly dubious, and anyway we are no longer at the origin; perhaps we are at the end. Though in our métier, the end, or the goal, consists of reaching the origin. And any origin will do, if it works. As for me, riding along on this personal and dubious epic of mediations, I have found the trends of Contemporary Art to be an unparalleled and inexhaustible source of productive fantasizing ever since my first exposure, which has a date. It was in 1967, in a bookstore in Buenos Aires, when I bought the book *Marchand du Sel*, the first compilation of the writings of Marcel Duchamp, edited by Michel Sanouillet. This book, published in 1959 by Éric Losfeld of Le Terrain Vague, contained a transparent foldout of a photograph of *The Large Glass* (1915–1923) and has since become a valuable collector's item—so much so that I had to buy a pocketbook edition so I could stop fondling it and be able to keep it in good condition in case I wanted to sell it one day. The contents of a book, along with its burden of quality and information, can be moved without loss from the gorgeous first edition to the cheap throwaway one. As opposed to an image, the written word did not need technological developments to achieve the perfect reproduction of itself.

But this is where we see the intervention of fetishism, which is the dialectical surpassing of reproduction. And it is because of a sentimental or autobiographical fetishism that for now I don't plan to sell my *Marchand du Sel*. At eighteen, when I bought it, I wanted to be a writer; I wanted to write novels like the ones that had accompanied me since childhood, offer opinions on my colleagues, type on my typewriter until I wore down my fingers, say intelligent and important things, be a poet, an essayist, win the Nobel Prize; moreover, and as if all that were a mere trifle, I felt I still had time to be Arthur Rimbaud. But the spell of Duchamp, that cold fascination to which he held the secret key, interrupted those plans forever. Mine was an intuition that had no definite shape but was impossible to ignore. The lack of definition surrounding it made it even more irresistible. After more than forty years, I have begun to discern what was behind that adolescent reverie, and I still don't know if it was exactly what I proposed, or if there can be anything exact in all this, or if it's important to understand it.

I believe that what was revealed to me, through that transparent foldout, was the futility of writing books, even loving them as I loved them, or precisely because I loved them. The time had come to do something else. That other thing (that anyway was already done and Duchamp had done it) was what I ultimately did, disguising myself as a writer in order to not have to explain myself: write the footnotes, the imaginary and irreverent though coherent and systematic instructions for certain mechanisms I invented, which made reality function to my benefit.

This plan was antidiscursive without failing to be loquacious. It satisfied both a taste for secrecy and a distaste for opportunistic silence; it saved me from speaking, explaining, interpreting, opining, teaching, communicating, but not writing, for it took writing out of the arena of a windbag's chatter and placed it on the same wavelength as games of intelligence and invention, through which Duchamp had passed and his abundant slipstream was passing, which shortly thereafter would come to be called Contemporary Art.

This background information undoubtedly exposes me as an assiduous reader of and subscriber to magazines that convey new developments in art: *Artforum*, first of all (my collection of *Artforum* goes back to the seventies), then *Art in America*, *Flash Art*, *Frieze*, *art press* ... And I begin with magazines because of something I have noticed, that many others will have noticed, and that becomes more notorious every year: these magazines, increasingly well produced, with always more perfect photographic reproductions, offer an increasingly impoverished and disheartening visual display. *Artforum* arrives and my first impatient glance encounters photographs of dark chambers with screens that show blurry images, empty galleries, a woman sitting at a table, garments hanging on coat stands, video footage where something that could be foliage or clouds or a puddle can just barely be discerned, a room with some wooden planks thrown on the floor or leaning against the walls, a snapshot of a family on a beach, a cocktail, an office ... It is possible to reach the last page without having found anything that visually speaks for itself. One must return to the beginning and read carefully in order to discover what those disappointing photographs were making reference to; and, once informed, one recognizes that they were the best possible documentation of works of art that might well be innovative, intelligent, and worthwhile, but that insist with headstrong determination to not allow themselves to be photographed.

Let us leave aside, for the moment, the usual criticism by the Enemy of Contemporary Art, who would say that today's frauds who pretend to be artists depend on a justifying discourse to validate the nonsense they produce. Let us instead think about the logic and history of reproduction—without getting into the philosophical issue of "aura," which, personally, I've never found very convincing. A work of art has always implicitly contained its own reproduction. By being exposed to perception and memory, ghosts are inevitably released into space and time. In that sense, a work of art is merely the model for its reproductions, and almost nothing more (otherwise, it is only an object of prestige, subject to all the mishaps and manipulations of any object). Moreover, concrete and tangible reproduction has always accompanied the work of art. The Greeks reproduced statues (and I remember my surprise when I read in Kenneth Clark's book that the originals were bronze and marble was used for the copies; I'd always thought it was the other way around). The prehistory of reproduction was the copy, made painstakingly, one at a time. But already in that prehistory there were molds and castings, from which a three-dimensional impression was made. With photography, the reproduction of a work of art achieved a state that could be called definitive, from then on admitting only to improvements. Though we can see that these improvements don't always work. Federico Zeri used to say that in his studies and research he used only black-and-white photographs, not only because of the poor quality of chemical color but also for reasons of formal structure. Perhaps we should review the history of the grisaille as a mnemonic device.

At a certain moment, precisely the moment of Contemporary Art, it is as if a race started between the work of art and the technical possibility of reproducing it. And it is perhaps this race, this flight forward, that dictates the form taken by the work of art. The work of Contemporary Art flees from technical reproduction to the extent that this advances, and improves. A work becomes a work of art today to the extent that it remains one step ahead of the possibility of its reproduction . . .

An eloquent avatar of this race was the installation, now a bit out of date but which left a mark that spread well beyond its format, strictly speaking. Photography can offer only a partial idea of an installation, and even something less than partial, for it situates it on the same plane as illustrations in an interior design magazine. Through their mechanism of entry, tour, and exit, installations mock reproduction in an insidious way: they are a trap, not only for the unwary. Commenting on an installation by Joseph Beuys, David Sylvester indicated the exact spot where the spectators should place themselves to obtain the best vantage point for an aesthetic and emotional appreciation of the work. A critic as perceptive as Sylvester but trained in the study and enjoyment of painting completely misunderstood the "installation" format, rescuing the possibility of its reproduction by indicating the spot where the object of the camera should be situated.

It is true that what could be called the "technology of reproduction" (or, of reproduction-representation-documentation) has been improved in recent decades through the incorporation of movement, sound, and—with digitalization—the possibility of compressing enormous quantities of information into a minimum amount of space. But this improvement responds to, and perhaps follows, previous steps taken by Contemporary Art to incorporate movement, sound, time in all its alterations, and encyclopedic information. The Contemporary Artist continues to move forward, taking one step after another, and employs her ingenuity and inventiveness to endow her work with one aspect, one side, one point, that remains hidden, even from the most novel and exhaustive technique of reproduction. Hence art magazines, if they wish to be truly up to date, must continue to be visually disappointing, for their illustrations must remain precisely one moment before they are able to give a comprehensive idea of the work.

This lack, small or large, in reproduction (and I am still referring to the photographs that illustrate my art magazines), this programmatically imperfect reproduction, suggests another work of art; the irreproducible point is there to generate not exactly a different work but rather a different story. I see, in an article about recent work by a young artist, the photograph of a pile of sand on the floor. What is the work? It could be sand from Sinai transported to a museum in Alaska, or the idea is for the spectators to spread it around, or sit on it, or each should take a grain, or it could be covering a Constantin Brancusi sculpture ... You cannot photograph a concept. But the text that explains it would also lack something, and something fundamental: it would lack that constellation of possible stories that glides over the naked photo. And the combination of photo and text, in a paradoxical downshifting, would be even more lacking.

What I want to say is that in this race they have started running, the work and its reproduction are so close upon each other's heels that they end up confounded. Reproduction becomes a work of art, or more precisely, art without work. "A dream not dreamed," Giorgio de Chirico said. A dream not yet dreamed, latent, without the arrogance of the achieved. Art becomes a slightly fantastical game with time: it is the documentation of something that was, and at the same time a promise of something that will be. Unborn and posthumous. Perhaps this has always been the work of art: a being of precarious and ambiguous existence, suspended between the before and the after, subservient to a script that conceals its beauty and enchantment like a secret.

After all, we have good reason to consider the concrete existence of works of art to be a bit shabby, with the prestige they offer to the semieducated, as a fishhook for tourists or millionaires, with their scornful immobility, their arrogance as expensive objects. That oft-repeated question, "What would you save from a fire in the Louvre?"— or the Prado, or MoMA—doesn't it reveal, because repetitive and classic, the pleasure it would give us to see a venerable institution enveloped in flames, to be finally released from the burden of that grab bag full of trinkets?

If the race between the work of art and its reproduction will always be won by the work, and won, thanks to advances in the technologies of reproduction, by an ever-decreasing margin, we have before us a new version of the race between Achilles and the tortoise. But a reproduction becomes a work of art, and the work of art a reproduction, when both understand that what is important is the story, the script of the fable, which moves both of them.

We would need to speak of "expanded reproduction," though not expanded along the line of technical improvements but rather expanded in all directions, or better still, in all dimensions, even the heterogeneous ones. And that would be literature, at least as I understand it, or have been understanding it since 1967—literature as "expanded reproduction," in all directions of a multidimensional continuum, of a work of art, which would have ceased to matter, or be pertinent, if it existed or not.

This story that I have constructed around Contemporary Art could be applied to any era. Perhaps the work of art always arranged things so that no reproduction could portray it fully. We should consider an extended concept of "aura" that would include the story that arises from the work. The concrete reality of the work would consist of the work itself and the time involved in its conception and execution, understanding this time as a historical unfolding, of which each aspect is unique and unrepeatable, and therefore irreproducible. Then nobody would give much credit to the banal advice to appreciate a work of art only for its plastic values, independent of the knowledge of associations that surround it. Not even the most dogmatic formalist, one who hangs a painting upside down in order to be able to focus on the play of shapes and colors, manages to wriggle out of one account or another. (Richard Wollheim has written with great insight on this subject.)

Only in the last several decades, however, with the advent of ever-improved technological means of reproduction, has this so conspicuously guarded secret about art come to light. Maintaining a quantum of irreproducibility became the task that indicated the direction art should take. This guaranteed that Contemporary Art would be—is—an art of formats, an epic of formats in flight.

I sometimes fantasize about inserting artists from the past into the sizzling present day of Contemporary Art. Not as a mere counterfactual game but rather in order to detect this bonus of hidden reality in their art. Indeed, artists from, let's say, the Renaissance, had limited formats (painting, drawing, sculpture). Within these limitations, some were able to leave the trace of their *Green Box*, and it is this trace that keeps them alive for us. Erudition brings to light these mechanisms when it adopts a certain innovative rhythm or impulse. In practical terms, this occurs when one can write about them in the past tense and not in the present used to describe paintings. Here's one example, taken from an essay about Nicolas Poussin by Mario Praz:

> [Poussin] resorted to a most surprising method.
> He first made a pencil and bistre sketch of the intended picture, then he modeled in wax all the figures of it, placing them exactly in their attitudes, first in the nude, then dressed as they had to appear, by help of coloured cambric, paper, or taffeta; he likewise modeled in wax the buildings and other paraphernalia; finally, he built round this kind of *presepio* a box with such openings to let in the light as there would be in the place for which the painting was designed. This method left nothing to chance. But it served not only the practical purpose of securing unity and coherence to the picture; through it Poussin satisfied his strong tactile instincts while actually moulding his figures, and at the same time, in contemplating them at once so distinct and so remote, as happens with miniature models of the *presepio*

kind, he treasured in his eyes an impression which translated itself into the spell-bound, entranced appearance of the finished picture. The charm of Poussin's pictures lies in their being imbued with the memory of a tactile experience, and in bathing for ever in the strange, almost aquarium light of a *presepio*. Poussin had actually seen with his bodily eyes, not only with those of his mind, the Roman, Greek, or Biblical scene he was painting; he had seen all the details of it, as they were at the time the historical event took place, he had in a way touched the bodies and the dresses of the personages. This method was almost that of an archaeological reconstruction; but the mind which devised it, while believing it satisfied only requirements of an erudite and scientific nature, was in fact indulging in the strangest of metaphysical yearnings: it drugged itself with method and technique in order to dream better.[1]

This smells intensely of Contemporary Art. Not because he built a diorama, something that had always been done, but rather because of that migration of the medium, among sculpture, painting, toy, miniature, ceremony, and ritual. The painted picture at the end is merely the visible testament to the mad solitary machine that moves around inside artistic activity. Poussin's

---

[1] Mario Praz, "Milton and Poussin," in *Seventeenth Century Studies Presented to Sir Herbert Grierson* (Oxford, UK: Clarendon Press, 1938), p. 204.

painting, in its exquisite workmanship, in the timeless-
ness of the museum, is the document, written in code, of
a story of experience, nostalgia, hallucination, in which
Mario Praz, Daniel Arasse, and others also play a part.

Before all this, one must ask oneself if it is really necessary to reproduce works of art, either in these magazines I await so eagerly or in any other medium. Because for centuries paintings and statues sat tight and waited for us to go see them. They behaved like ghosts, who speak only when spoken to and are eminently sedentary, more than death. And they did that because they counted on time for what they had been created to do, and they could wait. Contemporary Art, by wanting to be contemporary, has nullified time by compressing it into the present, and it must be everywhere at once. That's how the engine gets started: reproduction becomes necessary, the artist responds with her own need to hide something from reproduction, reproduction is improved so that art cannot hide anything from it … And that race, hurtling over the present moment, justifiably receives the name "contemporary."

In this situation, magazines advantageously replace books; the book had its reason to be in time, which imposed its own hierarchies. Magazines thrive in the dehierarchization of the instantaneous. Old art books, even Bernard Berenson, were travel guides that promised, usually in the suggestive rhetoric of tourist brochures, real visions of monuments anchored in space-time. Today, magazines, as well as exhibition catalogues (which, symptomatically, are never reissued), extend into the present a transmission network from an art world uncoupled from time. And it is a demanding transmission that seeks to become increasingly complete; this demand turns against itself when it is transmitted to artists, who will make it their duty to create something with some aspect or other that renders its reproduction incomplete. And not only its photographic or video reproduction, but also its written complement, signed by the Rosalind Krauss or Arthur Danto of the day. I am far from underestimating the abilities of the likes of Rosalind Krauss and Arthur Danto. On the contrary, I am certain that they can, if they wish, reveal the deepest secrets of a work of art, as they have readily shown. But that is precisely their limitation: among a work's secrets there is one, the most important one, which is not in the work and is inaccessible from the specific plane where the work occurs. Because the work is done, everything that refers to it will belong to some form of the past, to what is certain and shut.

All we'd have to do is eliminate Poussin's paintings and leave Poussin to see the appearance of the dimension of the not-done, which is where I believe the utopian secret of Contemporary Art resides. To incorporate the not-done into the done is the task that some artists seem to have taken on, from the very moment when the saga of modernism declared itself over. What is done—existing books, paintings, sculpture, videos, et cetera—due to the fact of having been done, are products, and as such are objects in the marketplace. And the bad part of this is that in order to function in the market, they must convey already established and confirmed values, thereby betraying the ultimate mission of art, which is to create new values and place them in circulation.

But the done continues and will continue to be the necessary support for the not-done, which resides in its material like a secret tale. Literature, or literature as I understand and practice it, could be the silver bridge hung between the done and the not-done, which establish between themselves a mysterious and suggestive asymmetry.

Another perspective on this same issue has to do with names. Someone at some point should create, if it doesn't already exist, a history or encyclopedia of the names of artistic movements. It's a story that lasted for approximately a century in its explicit form. It began with the impressionists, a name that, as would later happen with others such as cubism and fauvism, was born as a critique, or as ridicule. Others were programmatic names, such as futurism; others were provocative, such as Dada; still others were descriptive, such as expressionism; abstract, geographic, such as the School of Paris; others were acronyms, such as CoBrA. In the sixties, there was an explosive acceleration; names, and what they designated, proliferated: pop, op, minimalism, conceptualism, land art, photorealism, arte povera, and hundreds more. Like all explosions of form, this one laid waste; from then on, there would be no names. The few that were later proposed, such as pattern painting, or bad painting, or Die Neue Wilden (new fauves)—all in the seventies—or the transavantgarde, were fleeting and limited. The carnival of names had shut down; there barely remained an ersatz placing of "neo" or "post" in front of an old name.

This shouldn't have been a problem: art could have continued to function without names as it had for centuries. However, the big art auction houses needed a name to put on the products they had for sale and on the covers of their catalogues; so they reached a consensus and without entering into any of the residual categories decided to give a conventional name to everything that had been produced after 1970. The name they chose, without straining their brains and with a meager vision of the future, was Contemporary Art. A perfectly absurd name, not descriptive, or provocative, or geographic, and astonishingly neutral, almost a parody.

Curiously, however, the name took, and stayed, and through its very permanence, which in and of itself is paradoxical, it has begun to make sense; among other things, or principally, because everything it designates, even in its enormous variety, shares common features, a certain shared atmosphere, which is its coexistence in a historical moment that ludicrously renounces History and spreads itself out as a permanent present.

They say that the concept of "art" arose in the eighteenth century. Nobody has finally agreed on a description of the concept. In my judgment, it would be a constraint that isolates the small active part of what before, or always, has been called "art," and relegates all the rest to the category of craft. This—craft—must be done well (in order for it to be accepted, appreciated, and sold). To do it well, it is necessary to do it as it has always been done, to accommodate it to a canon that admits only to variations, and these only within acceptable margins. Art, on the other hand, isn't art if it's done well (that is, if it submits to already established values). It's not necessary to do art well—and making an effort to do so is a lamentable waste of time, which young people often fall into. If it is art, or for it to be art, it should create new values; it doesn't need to be good, on the contrary: if it can be called good that means it's obeying already fixed parameters of quality, and so can be placed, according to this novel eighteenth-century concept reinterpreted by me, in the category of "craft."

I would push back the start date to when there began to be names for schools or movements, that is, to impressionism, or its "precursors," in the Borgesian sense. It is then, when it becomes aware of itself, that it becomes a creator of values, or in less portentous terms, of taste parameters. Time, historical time, begins to take part in the game. It is what we have agreed to call modernism, or modernity: a teleology pointing at the future, which had its noisiest figures in the avant-gardes. This process culminated in the 1960s, and then it stopped.

Contemporary Art could be the realization of the teleology of modernism. It no longer pretends to herald the future, the future becoming of time, but is instead a smooth and flat realization of the present.

"To create values" is to intervene in the personal history of the spectator: to create taste, offer a new gaze … This has, or has had, its equivalent in the artist: from the moment art ceases to see itself as the production of beautifully crafted objects, it passes into the dimension of the not-done, and art objects become only what props up the biographical myth of the artist. As soon as the original idea becomes intelligible, it can do without the objects, and in fact usually does do without them, or degrades them, or pulls them out of the garbage. The object becomes secondary to the story from which it emerges. In this way, the artist shows consistency with the eighteenth-century concept, for to create values is to tell stories.

The creation of values by art occurs in History; moreover, it is an epiphenomenon of History. Art historians must carry out delicate archeological labor in order to discern the reigning values (aesthetic or other) at any particular moment in order to discern the exact contribution an artist makes to the table of values.

But, then . . . as art moves, as it seems to have, onto a plateau of permanent contemporaneity, the creation of values becomes contiguous with its perception in taste. That's why Contemporary Art has no detractors of specific details but rather generalized, massive enemies; there is no historical (temporal) gap so that a taste developed at one stage is confronted with a taste developed at the next, because there are no longer stages, successive or skipped over, but rather one unique plane of shrunken time, contemporary with itself. Time has become space, and in Contemporary Art you're either in or you're out.

The characters who revolve around the Contemporary Artist (curators, critics, et cetera), together comprising Contemporary Art, find themselves facing that paradoxical situation of discerning the historical development of values . . . outside of History. History is a selection and is therefore a brake on proliferation. Freed from this brake, Contemporary Art proliferates, vast and myriad. In the most remote village in Thailand or Argentina someone is watching on YouTube Paul McCarthy's latest fantasy, or a performance by Marina Abramović; thousands of artists are showing in small or large galleries, in large museums, or in their own garages. Common sense tells us that the passage of time will make its demanding selection and only the good will remain, or better said, what will remain is what has managed to create a new parameter of quality that we can use to decide from then on what is good and what isn't. But in Contemporary Art, there is no passage of time if it is really "contemporary," or in other words, if contemporaneity is what makes it art. There's no need to await the judgment of History to establish value because this new kind of art that is called Contemporary Art is its own documentation—it is writing its own history simultaneously with its appearance and doesn't need time to pass.

One of the traditional barriers to proliferation was the long and difficult apprenticeship to learn artistic technique. Today, those barriers have fallen. To learn the laws of perspective, or how to sculpt or polish marble, or make oil glazes, is merely one further eccentricity that some will undertake in their search for originality, and not at all necessary. On the one hand, we could deplore this to the extent that pseudoartists appear on the scene and thrive merely because of this current ease. On the other hand, it brings up the long-awaited possibility that there will appear and we will finally meet the Mozarts and Rimbauds of the arts, who in other epochs would have remained unknown and without a body of work because they did not have the patience to undergo an apprenticeship or had no access to one. Film is rapidly approaching the situation of Contemporary Art. I remember many years ago an Argentine director said: "When film ceases to be a heavy industry, expensive and cumbersome, when making a movie will be as easy as picking up a pencil and writing a poem, only then will film become a full-fledged art, and everything prior to that will be seen as poignant prehistory."

This reflects, of course, a lot of utopian and wishful thinking. Perhaps the facts will prove the contrary, that the obstacles of technique and studies and financing are integral and essential parts of the art of the cinema. And, mutatis mutandis, it's not unthinkable that the laborious initial crafts of painting and sculpture are essential to the plastic arts.

One important cog of Contemporary Art—I would even call it fundamental—is the militant Enemy of Contemporary Art, who argues and rants against the fraud perpetrated by these bums who have become millionaires thanks to the snobbery of the masses, who writes books with titles that tend to be variations on *It's All Duchamp's Fault*, and who lashes out at examples of ridiculous works of art ("art" in quotes) in Contemporary Art. This last requires no effort: examples abound, and they abound so much that one might suspect that they are being dished up to him on platters, or that they are being made specifically for him. After Duchamp's urinal, almost any work of Contemporary Art removed from its context, its history, the explanation surrounding it, lends itself to sardonic description. More than lends itself: it could be said that it was created as the object of sardonic description, and that this description is something like the zero degree of its reception. Without reaching that first rung, its reception cannot take flight.

In discussions fostered by the Enemy of Contemporary Art, the argument is usually propped up by imaginary examples created by his aggressive fantasy, such as "Nobody is going to convince me that hanging condoms full of shit from the ceiling is art." Those listening—even if they know the example is a creation of the moment, under the influence of strong convictions—likely wonder if that work of art (with or without quotes) might have once been created. And if it wasn't created, it could have been, or it will be, because that logic of a defamatory imaginary example—a form of "whatever"—is at the origins of creativity.

The defamatory example is more than just the favorite weapon of the Enemy of Contemporary Art. It is latent in the nucleus of proliferation. It is a promise of realization beyond the realities, foreseeable and planned, of reasonable evolution. It opens the way for true, nonderivative creation. (We must also keep in mind that defamation, when it is done well, has its own way of maturing into praise, vindication, or authentic comprehension; one example of this is *Candide* [1759] by Voltaire, written to mock Gottfried Leibniz's theory of preestablished harmony, which we can read today as the most convincing illustration of that theory.)

This is where the "whatever" formula comes from, which can be taken as a formula for freedom as well as irresponsibility. I prefer the first, and I am an ardent defender, in the literature that I write and the art that I appreciate, of "whatever" as the open sesame of creativity. I suppose it is also legitimate to see this as an indicator of frivolous irresponsibility if the purpose is to give art and literature some kind of conventional social belonging.

An example of a "whatever" that went from defamatory or self-defamatory to "museum quality," not exactly of Contemporary Art but incomparably illustrative, is René Magritte's so-called *vache* period. It happened in 1948 and was the result of specific circumstances, which shows that the full spectrum of possibilities in "whatever" requires the contrary—a combination of very precise causes—to occur. Magritte, already a well-known and appreciated artist in Belgium in 1948, was invited to hold an exhibition in Paris for the first time. With his friend Louis Scutenaire, the Belgian surrealist poet, he decided to show works that did not fit the image that had begun to be associated with him (or any other image, for that matter). He chose a different style, whereby the popular prejudice of the French that the Belgian were brutish animals prevailed through sarcasm, to which was added the provocation of not falling into the cliché of the provincial Belgian's reverence to the prestige of Paris. So, within a few weeks, one or two a day, he painted the seventeen oil paintings and twenty-two gouaches that would comprise the exhibition. Based on the premise of mocking French critics and amateurs, he had permission to do "whatever," liberated from the restrictions of quality, métier, or meaning. Paintings clumsily framed, of men with ten pipes embedded in their faces or the barrel of a rifle for a nose, a rhinoceros climbing up a column, a fugitive with a wooden leg chasing a red hen, a man-foot, a woman licking her shoulder, a sky of Scottish plaid ... Rarely in the History of Art has there been such a combination of circumstances so favorable to the emergence of all the possibilities latent in the formulation of images.

After the exhibition, Magritte returned to Belgium and left the paintings in the garret of a house in Paris, considering them of no importance whatsoever. They had served their purpose of carrying out his joke, and once this was accomplished they no longer interested him. This gesture showed Magritte to be consistent in his intention to escape from the established parameters of value. We would have to wait forty-four years for them to be gathered together again, at an exhibition at the Musée Cantini in Marseilles in 1992. The catalogue for this exhibition, which has not been reissued, is the other irreplaceable jewel of my library. More than a catalogue of an exhibition, it is the catalogue of what can appear on the surface of the not-done when this is given total freedom, which is what the artist should look for. All other paintings in the world had come about as a result of a conditioned process, in which restrictions rose out of psychology, taste, history, or society. The machinations of a joke were needed in order for the magma of the not-done to become a truly limitless totality, and it was from there that the thirty-nine paintings emerged. Each one of them contains that totality, in the form of freedom.

Inverting the formula of the libertines, Magritte said: "If I am allowed to do everything . . ." The consequences remain a blank, or are occupied by this marvelous combination, a monument *avant la lettre* to the "operational" character of Contemporary Art. Everything should be allowed so that what arises out of that everything has the liberating value we should demand of art. In the visitor book of the 1948 exhibit, Paul Éluard, displeased like all his surrealist friends by the Belgian's savage mockery, wrote: "He who laughs last, laughs best." He made a mistake to involve time, for in Contemporary Art, which is where Magritte's *vache* paintings are genuinely salvaged, nobody knows who will laugh before or after because historical perspective has vanished and values are in permanent gestation. It is as if Magritte, through that operation, had fulfilled the goal of Contemporary Art before Contemporary Art and under conditions that in Contemporary Art could not exist, for by that time, after 1970, that magma of "whatever" would have risen to the surface and what was emerging would be confounded with its unrealized possibilities.

I wonder if literature could do something equivalent. Freedom is also, or is in the first instance, the freedom to not please. But I think it would be very difficult for literature, because the entire effect Magritte achieved was based on the brutal quantum of the presence of paintings, a presence that in literature is mediated by meaning.

But the Enemy of CA is merely one piece of a conglomerate in which many people other than the artist participate. That's precisely where the Enemy of Contemporary Art finds the basis for one of his arguments: the artist has become one of many cogs, and not even the most important one, in an apparatus that consists of curators, gallery owners, collectors, assistants, critics, and even investment consultants. He should add himself as an essential member of the scheme. But it has always been like that, there were always patrons, commissions, disciples. If now that marginal apparatus seems more important, more densely populated, it is because the work of the artist remains incomplete without it. From the moment the work doesn't close itself up as a product, it can incorporate everything around it; to begin with, it incorporates the artist herself, and once the door has opened it is difficult to close it again.

One argument the reviling of CA is usually based on, in fact the central argument touted by the Enemy of Contemporary Art, is that the work of art today doesn't hold up without the discourse wrapped around it and justifying it. It does not "speak for itself" but rather requires seasoned ventriloquists, usually critics or curators.

At the beginning was Duchamp; it could almost be said that he was the origin myth, and like all myths, he was not only the first mover but the one who blazes the entire path, and one can only keep walking back and forth along it—with the peculiarity that his discourse was his own and was explicitly part of his work. This is not to say that afterwards the critics, curators, and historians didn't endlessly embroider around the work, but he was the inventor of a work of art that consisted of two inseparable parts: the work and the discourse about the work. *The Large Glass* and *The Green Box* (1934) were, or was, in singular, the first and definitive essay. Later improved upon with the readymades, and in the direction of the most terse and elegant simplicity: in the readymade, the work is whatever, the discourse is only the signature of the artist.

It's curious to note the symmetry of opposition, on this point, between Duchamp and Salvador Dalí, who were friends, admired each other, and between whose respective work many affinities have been found. Duchamp didn't care if the work was made by somebody else, or not made by anybody, or was bought in a bazaar, as long as the discourse that supported it was his and nobody's but his (as his signature came to be, on its own; this is confirmed by the fact that with *The Green Box* he made an effort to reproduce his manuscripts in facsimile, so as not to leave any doubt to the absolute ownership of his words). Dalí, on the other hand, had no problem with many of his books being written by others, or composed by others from his notes, which were written in shaky handwriting and worse syntax. But his pictorial work was intensely his, using techniques from the Renaissance of intense physical and temporal charge.

Dalí didn't care that his books were written by others because of the system he had previously created, which is summed up in one of his characteristic declarations: "Whoever thinks about Dalí will have brilliant ideas, whoever writes about Dalí will write brilliant things, whoever buys Dalís will become wealthy." Within the myth of genius (it's also characteristic that he would furnish genius with wealth) Dalí brings together work and discourse, and if it is Duchamp who offers the practical recipe for the Contemporary Artist, I think it is Dalí who gives the Duchampian system its highest polish by consummating both worlds: the instantaneity of the signature and the extended pleasure of the work. Duchamp did try the game of craftsmanship, though, especially in *Étant donnés* (1946–1966), to which, significantly, he offered no accompanying discourse.

This is very suggestive if placed, like a transparency, over literature. It is more difficult for literature to establish the duplicity between work and discourse because it is already a discourse. In any case, the question is other: Why does contemporary literature not have its own enemy? Why does there not exist an Enemy of Contemporary Literature? Perhaps because there doesn't exist anything that has been institutionalized as "contemporary literature." But this can be circular. If there doesn't exist a "contemporary literature" labeled as such, it might well be because it doesn't have a specific enemy that has shaped it in the negative through their indignation and sarcasm.

Perhaps literature has an inherent difficulty being "contemporary." As opposed to Art—which has such a heightened presence that it creates its own present, whether because of "aura" or some other question—literature has a material made instead from absence; and as far as time, it creates its own past, its own precursors, perhaps because it is always talking about vanished worlds, and the only value writers ask for is that: to be the only visible trace of a great shipwreck, the beauty of the world.

There is also a more concrete reason. What mainly fuels the indignation of the Enemy of Contemporary Art is the millions of dollars the artist makes with a sleight of hand. But the writer who is equivalent to that kind of artist, the radical and experimental writer, doesn't earn millions. The one who does earn millions is the author of best sellers, but in that case he earns it through the sweat of his brow because he has learned his métier and practices it conscientiously; best sellers are nineteenth-century novels constructed by dint of skill and métier, and they are also very long. No Enemy of the Contemporary would have anything to reproach them for.

Money carries social legitimization, and the oceans of money that flow toward Contemporary Art, and the portentous social legitimization that follows, promote a climate of festive, shared work, which, if we had to search for a parallel in literature, could be found in writers' residencies, workshops, clinics, fairs, colloquia, high-end tourism, and experiences that promote creativity. Secret, individual, ascetic creation carried out in order to somehow alleviate a lack of adaptation or the difficulty of being alive was a specialty of literature, which the plastic arts did not share, at least not as a general characteristic. And when an artist worked in solitude and in secret in order to alleviate a lack of adaptation and the difficulty of being alive, she did it because she was also, and previously, a writer. As was the case with Henry Darger.

Perhaps now, in the wake of the unbridled institutionalization of Contemporary Art, literature is moving in the direction of the same kind of legitimization, and is turning into a euphoric parade of inventiveness, like Contemporary Art today. In that case, the ill-adapted, marginalized, and individualist diehards will have to find other means of expression. Which is perhaps a good thing, as we already have a lot of literature.

It is not necessary to invent an ad hoc example of a secret, ascetic, individualistic work of literature, as we know it—that's what Kafka is for. What I want to show about this asymmetrical parallelism between literature and Contemporary Art can be seen in the following fable. Let us suppose that Franz Kafka had not existed, and that a group of writers, through an experiment in literary creativity, writes *The Castle*, *The Metamorphosis*, and "Josephine the Singer, or the Mouse Folk" exactly, down to the last word, just as in the real world Kafka wrote it. Would it have the same value for us? Apparently not, because the most important part would be missing: Kafka. And if we want to know what that Kafka element is, we have no choice but to conclude that the

essential condiment is historic: a man living in History—
unrepeatable, noninterchangeable, and crucial. This is
what makes it so difficult and painful for him, and he
needs to create his work in order to get out of the ago-
nizing impasse.

Maybe I'm taking a name, which is merely a conven-
tion in the art market, too seriously, though the universal
acceptance of that name permits certain speculations.
The installation of the Contemporary implies a negation
of History, at least History as a provider of biographical
myths that sustain literary value. A liberating negation,
maybe. Because what I said a moment ago about literature is also valid here: Who needs new values? Who
needs values?

To end where I began.

We must agree with the Enemy of Contemporary Art on one thing, that it's Duchamp's fault. His work lay dormant for half a century, for as long as the impulse born with Édouard Manet and Paul Cézanne lasted, until the 1960s, when his rediscovery by artists such as Jasper Johns, Robert Rauschenberg, and others concurred with a natural approximation of his work on the part of new trends including pop, minimalism, and the Happening, perhaps the consequence (only perhaps: I am not an art historian) of the depletion of the Manet-Cézanne impulse. Since then, we have had Contemporary Art. Except Contemporary Art, with all its rich and, for me, fascinating diversity, refutes its own name, because it is, to a large extent, the art of the past: the past of Duchamp's life.

Duchamp is another example of the Law of Diminishing Returns, about which I have written more than once. I quote myself:

If we have a metal spring one meter long with one end on the ground and we place a one-kilo weight on the other end of the spring, the spring will descend ninety centimeters and measure barely ten centimeters high. To make it shorter, one hundred kilos more would be needed, which would lower it nine centimeters. To make it descend a fraction more of that remaining centimeter, a weight of more than several tons would be needed.... The same can be applied to intellectual work. Euclid writes his *Elements* in a few days, or a few hours; the work of thousands of geometricians for two thousand years has just barely added minor and marginal advances. Examples of this type abound: Freud, the discoverer of the unconscious: one hundred years of the dedicated work of disciples and followers haven't managed to substantially enhance his work, and every pretense of progress has to occur under the guise of a "return to Freud."

A field that opens in the sciences or the humanities offers itself entirely to the one who has opened it. It's not so certain that this applies to the arts. Maybe in the case of schools or movements that had names. The first impressionist did all of impressionism, the first fauvist, the first cubist … It's true that in the case of cubism there were two, but they were melded into one, and anyway, there were only two. Even so, cubism is a good example: everything was done in two years, and Albert Gleizes and Jean Metzinger and Juan Gris, who wanted to continue doing it, could not have found any more efficient way to be nullified. I have always been disheartened by the prodigious intellectual effort required in order to generate a gram of enthusiasm for Juan Gris.

But Contemporary Art, that thing that has reigned and proliferated since 1970, seems like a machine designed to disprove the Law of Diminishing Returns. And it does so, not by denying the mechanism of the Law, but rather by accepting it and putting it to work in its favor.

The recourse was to create the myth of Duchamp, and from there to find in his work the model or idea of everything that is done or that can be done. It is not objectively true that Duchamp has done everything, but this can be upheld with a little bit of ingenuity and by employing not only the artifacts created by Duchamp but also his gestures, anecdotes, and all available biographical details. Then one can affirm that "Duchamp already did it," and what the Contemporary Artist does is add a tiny fraction of 0.01 percent to the 99.99 percent that Duchamp covered. But that minimum, precisely because it is a minimum, leaves a lot of free space to continue doing. There has been an atomization that looks like liberation, and room for maneuvering has opened up on a scale never seen before. No longer does anything get in the way or create obstacles because of its size; the entire debate occurs among minimums. There are no more Picassos, no more anguish about influences. The exceptionality of genius remains encapsulated in a single figure in the past, leaving the present free for the shifting motions of a constellation of partial and provisional exceptionalities.

2010

Afterword

Alexandra Kleeman

When I arrived, the line was already so long that it stretched all the way down the block, where it turned a corner and proceeded down a side street, trailing just past the end of that block as well. The effect was unsettling: with the narrowness of the sidewalk and the length of the street, it was impossible to see any point where the line might end, any signs of it faltering. I'd often thought that the lines in this city are one of its greatest attractions, that we have the longest lines and the most numerous, fantastic lines, charged with raw human energy, full of life and also the resignation to patient waiting. I often said this aloud to others, while waiting in line. The day was warm and loud and crowded with light. Turning the final corner, I inserted myself behind a man reading a magazine article about the thing that we had all come here to see.

This particular line led to the entrance of a museum, within which the recently deceased artist's final installation could be found. It's impossible to know how long this line might have been if she were still alive—perhaps only to the end of the first block. In light of the artist's recent passing, essays and think pieces about her work had made her the subject of regular conversation, even parody. But as her persona grew more visible, more broadly heralded and celebrated, it became difficult to tell what exactly this final work was about, or even what its physical components might be. In articles that recapitulated an entire career, the final installation was sometimes called a "culmination" or an "aberration," and there were hints that it alluded somehow to death, or was perhaps entirely about death, but nothing certain could be gleaned from the description. And then there were, of course, the hundreds or even thousands of selfies taken within the installation and hashtagged with the artist's name, grainy and poorly lit faces grimacing in the half-light, their features distorted by the short distance to the lens and the unnatural angle, making cheekbones too large, foreheads too big, eyes crossed or flat or unfocused. In each, the foregrounding of self makes the installation in the background impossible to make out, a patterning of lights or the outline of something large and bulbous, obscure and not photogenic.

After an hour with no movement other than that of the occasional body quietly leaving the line to walk out into the larger, nonlinear world, we began to talk to one another. The man ahead of me had seen an early work by the artist thirty-five years ago. As he had entered the exhibition space, he saw three small plants in the center of the room, frail-looking plants adorned with a few floppy green leaves. They were oak saplings, thin as twigs, swaying momentarily in a gallery breeze too slight for human skin to sense. Reading the information on the wall, he realized that all three saplings were clones, and that a map on the far wall marked the location of ninety-seven others, which were growing in Ohio and Kentucky, Taipei, Sapporo, and Hamburg. It would be inaccurate to say that it was the trees that had made him cry—instead it was something more like the *number* of trees, or maybe the force of their sameness repeated one hundred times over, or maybe the space between the trees, a forest stretched too far and wide to ever come together again, the family structure lost. Today, thirty-five years later, some of those saplings must be small trees, modestly branching and casting small shade. Many others must be dead. In any case, he was hoping for something similar from this installation, he was ready to cry again if he had to, he had seen the faces of the museumgoers as they exited the building with somber expressions and he felt certain that there was something inside the exhibition of immense significance, something heartbreaking. He thought that maybe it was the artist's corpse, put on display, a sort of final transubstantiation of the physical body into an afterlife of images.

The woman behind me spoke up. The idea of featuring the artist's own dead body in the final installation seemed far too grim for someone whose work she had always described as, first and foremost, "playful." To her, the work was never about monumental existence, it was about mutation, chance, giving birth to monsters. One summer she had been living above a Venetian canal with a boyfriend whose family owned a large house, bought before they had lost their fortune. Every day, they walked through the narrow streets to a small square where one of the artist's installations sat beneath a large red awning. There, in the center of the square, the artist had laid down a shallow wooden frame and filled it with sand. Etched into the sand's smooth surface was the complete synopsis of "The Last One," the final episode of the television series *Friends*, an episode that received a record 52.3 million viewers the night it was aired.

Though the awning kept the sand more or less safe from rain, the etched forms slumped, the wind overwrote words and even entire phrases. At the end of each day, the artist reconstructed the synopsis as best she could, tracing over what the shapes seemed to say, and then a leaflet was issued bearing the latest version of the text. As the woman passed by each day, the synopsis grew stranger and stranger, taking on the syntax of ancient poetry. For a while it was a tale about a group of donkeys, then the donkeys too disappeared into a beautiful stew of words, sometimes more related than others. On the final day of the installation, a group of actors performed a theatrical interpretation of what was left of the text. But what she noticed as she visited the exhibition was that her boyfriend never seemed to look at the work for very long, never read more than a few words of the text before looking away, restless. Once she had noticed this behavior, she began to see it everywhere—in the books he started but quickly set aside, in the way he ordered from menus after only a glance, in the fact that she never caught him looking at her—and she began to feel that there was something doomed and irreparable about his incuriosity. After that summer, she never saw him again.

It had been hours, and the line had barely moved. We discussed this, considered whether something might have gone wrong or broken down within the exhibition, some emergency so urgent that no one had yet found the time to tell those waiting to disperse. Another possibility was that whatever was inside was so absorbing, so wondrous, that nobody who made their way in was willing to leave. We argued over whether visits to a Great Work should have an imposed time limit, whether contemporary art was the kind of "democratic" defined by a work's accessibility to all, or by freedom to choose what you do in its presence. Around us the city grew restless and then calmed itself again. Every so often one of us threatened to leave, even announcing this to our neighbors while stepping just slightly out of line before reluctantly folding ourselves back in.

But privately it occurred to me that perhaps the line we were standing in was the point of the whole thing. Our line, like a swaddling cloth, encircled the entire work and set it apart from the busy metropolitan background. From within it, we generated an aura of anticipation that colored the world rosily. We set in motion stories about the work's contents, just as we would have done had we made it inside to see it—and these stories were unrecorded, not transcribed, irreproducible, the ghostly effects of the absent object. In this sense, the work generated experience within us, narrative experience, even if it refused to be made available to us as stimulus. Even as the work withdrew, it had its effect.

As the afternoon turned to early evening and the streetlights clicked on, I saw the artist's last work clearly in my mind: a living, moving frame of human material, a line as a circle, breathing and stirring only slightly, incessantly pondering the unknown work at its center. There was no need to move forward, no need to reach our destination. We could remain here indefinitely, shifting from foot to foot, filtering in and out, replacing each other, uttering stories that were sometimes predictable, sometimes profound. It was enough to fill a whole day or several. And so I turned in the deepening dusk to the next person in line, a young woman who had said nothing all day, and asked her: What do you think is inside?

CÉSAR AIRA was born in Coronel Pringles, Argentina, in 1949 and has lived in Buenos Aires since 1967. He taught at the University of Buenos Aires and at the University of Rosario, and has translated and edited books from different languages. Perhaps one of the most prolific writers in Argentina and certainly one of the most talked about in Latin America, Aira has published more than 120 books. Rights to his books have been sold in almost thirty countries. One novel, *La prueba* (1992), has been made into a feature film. In 1996 he received a Guggenheim scholarship, in 2002 he was shortlisted for the Rómulo Gallegos International Novel Prize, in 2015 he was shortlisted for the Man Booker International Prize, and in 2016 he was guest of honor at the International Literature Festival Berlin and was awarded the Premio Iberoamericano de Narrativa Manuel Rojas.

KATHERINE SILVER is an award-winning literary translator and the former director of the Banff International Literary Translation Centre. Her most recent and forthcoming translations include works by María Sonia Cristoff, Horacio Castellanos Moya, Julio Cortázar, Juan Carlos Onetti, and Julio Ramón Ribeyro.

WILL CHANCELLOR is the author of the novel *A Brave Man Seven Storeys Tall* (2014). He has exhibited conceptual sculpture for the New Museum's Festival of Ideas for the New City (2011) and The Bellwether (2017). Currently he is working on a novel set in 1970s Russia titled *The Meaning of Certain Dreams*.

ALEXANDRA KLEEMAN is the author of the novel *You Too Can Have A Body Like Mine* and the story collection *Intimations* (both 2016). Her work has been published in *The New Yorker*, *The Paris Review*, *Harper's*, *Conjunctions*, and *n+1*, among other outlets. She lives in Staten Island and teaches at The New School.

Something Close to Music
John Ashbery

The Salon of 1846
Charles Baudelaire

My Friend Van Gogh
Émile Bernard

Strange Impressions
Romaine Brooks

A Balthus Notebook
Guy Davenport

That Still Moment
Edwin Denby

Ramblings of a Wannabe Painter
Paul Gauguin

Thrust: A Spasmodic Pictorial History of the Codpiece in Art
Michael Glover

Visions and Ecstasies
H.D.

Mad about Painting
Katsushika Hokusai

Blue
Derek Jarman

Kandinsky: Incarnating Beauty
Alexandre Kojève

Pissing Figures 1280–2014
Jean-Claude Lebensztejn

The Psychology of an Art Writer
Vernon Lee

Degas and His Model
Alice Michel

28 Paradises
Patrick Modiano and Dominique Zehrfuss

Any Day Now: Toward a Black Aesthetic
Larry Neal

Summoning Pearl Harbor
Alexander Nemerov

Chardin and Rembrandt
Marcel Proust

Letters to a Young Painter
Rainer Maria Rilke

The Cathedral Is Dying
Auguste Rodin

Giotto and His Works in Padua
John Ruskin

Duchamp's Last Day
Donald Shambroom

Dix Portraits
Gertrude Stein

Photography and Belief
David Levi Strauss

The Critic as Artist
Oscar Wilde

Oh, to Be a Painter!
Virginia Woolf

Two Cities
Cynthia Zarin

On Contemporary Art
César Aira

Translated from the Spanish
Sobre el arte contemporáneo

Published by
David Zwirner Books
520 West 20th Street, 2nd Floor
New York, New York 10011
+ 1 212 727 2070
davidzwirnerbooks.com

Editor: Lucas Zwirner
Project Manager: Mary Huber
Translator: Katherine Silver
Copy Editor: Deirdre O'Dwyer
Proofreader: Michael Ferut

Design: Michael Dyer / Remake
Production Manager: Jules Thomson
Printing: VeronaLibri, Verona

Typeface: Arnhem
Paper: Holmen Book Cream,
80 gsm

Publication © 2018
David Zwirner Books

First published 2018. Second
printing 2024

On Contemporary Art © César Aira
2018, published in arrangement
with Gaeb & Eggers Literary Agency,
Berlin

Foreword © 2018 Will Chancellor
Afterword © 2018 Alexandra Kleeman
Translation © 2018 Katherine Silver

Distributed in the United States
and Canada by
Simon & Schuster, Inc.
1230 Avenue of the Americas
New York, New York 10020
simonandschuster.com

Distributed outside the
United States and Canada by
Thames & Hudson, Ltd.
181A High Holborn
London WC1V 7QX
thamesandhudson.com

ISBN 978-1-941701-86-7

Library of Congress
Control Number: 2018946900

Printed in Italy